The Little Red Library

No. 4.

Worker Correspondents

WHAT **?** WHERE
WHEN WHY
HOW

By WILLIAM F. DUNNE.

PRICE 10 CENTS

PUBLISHED FOR

THE WORKERS PARTY OF AMERICA

BY

The Daily Worker Publishing Co.

CHICAGO, ILL.

Worker Correspondents by William F. Dunne

originally published in 1925 in Chicago by the Daily Worker Publishing Co.

REPRINTED by NEW OUTLOOK PUBLISHERS in 2019

ISBN 978-0-359-42165-7

Published by
New Outlook Publishers, Inc.

Dedication

We dedicate this to all Cadre who believe with their hearts, minds, and actions in a true New Outlook Revolution!

For one to be true, one must desire wholeheartedly, without reservation, to free themselves and their fellow workers from the bonds of class antagonisms. One who understands the foundations of Marxist-Leninist teachings, understands that their sole purpose in life is to crush capitalism.

We dedicate this reprint of an old classic in hopes that the truths expounded in this book and others will inspire you to take Communism to the next level, using the past expressions of scientific research into the nature of Marxism while adapting it to today's culture.

Remember, Marxist-Leninist ideals are scientific, so put on your "lab coat" do some research of old classics, and begin your new experiments for democratic-socialism.

We hope this book will inspire the reader to join the ranks of cadre working for a better tomorrow for all!

The Revolutionary Role of Worker Correspondents

By William F. Dunne

Section 1

Worker correspondents differ from professional journalists in that they are part of the labor and revolutionary movement and fight actively in the struggles of which they write.

The wider the activity of a worker correspondent in the class struggle, the greater will be the field covered by his reports. At first the worker correspondent ·will find it hard to gather material. As a worker, ordinary, daily events of development of the class struggle are familiar to him. He expects these. things as the routine of working class life and sees no news value in them.

It is this outlook of the worker that makes it hard for him to write or speak. He is not in articulate because of lack of words, but because he has been taught by capitalism to look upon the thousand and one tyrannies, inconveniences and hardships inflicted on the workers as of little importance-things to be endured without comment or complaint.

The countless risks of industry, the accidents to and deaths of workers, even great disasters taking a huge toll of working class lives, quite often cause less excitement among the workers than among the liberal middle class.

Why is this?

Because among the workers, deaths and accidents are common things to be expected as part of the price paid for being allowed to work.

This is the idea drilled into the mass mind by capitalists and especially by capitalist journalism. The death of the wealthy idler will get the first page and a streamer headline, but the death of a worker is either not mentioned at all or given a half dozen lines.

Journalism is recording and expressing opinion on contemporary events. Journalism, like everything else in capitalist society, is a class enterprise.

Journalism is the day by day listing of the facts of industry and politics and an analysis of those facts.

Journalism is therefore a class affair just the same as politics, industry, art and education.

The ruling class puts its stamp on journalism just as it stamps every other form of social activity. It can even be said that more than in any other from of social expression are the class lines apparent in journalism.

Not only does the clearly class character of the capitalist press become obvious to the class conscious worker, but the most casual observation shows that every division and subdivision of the social organism has its journalistic expression.

The capitalist press itself shades off into innumerable organs of separate groups-employers' and bankers' associations, trade associations, clubs, special organizations ·for suppression of the workers, all have their own publications.

The middle class has countless journals which cater to and express the opinions of some particular group.

Church newspapers and magazines are legion. In addition to these journals speaking openly, for some vested interest, there are the special propaganda organs 'of the ruling class-each with its own field.

All of these journals are anti-working class in character-some of them frankly so, some of them thinly disguised with the veil of humanitarianism, and "social welfare."

Then there are the official organs of the trade union movement and its various sections and affiliated bodies-formally opposing the capitalist but actually ruled by the ethics and swayed by the prejudices of capitalism.

The trade union press of the United States is not a labor press (with a few negligible exceptions) . It is in reality an aid to capitalism with its warfare on the communist Party, its espousal of imperialism, its catering to ignorant prejudices, its imitation of capitalist journalism and its middle class doctrine of "equality of opportunity and identity of interest."

The Socialist press joins with the official trade union press, apologizing for capitalism, praising its parliamentary system and fighting the Communist Party as well as every revolutionary tendency in the working class movement.

There remains the Communist press and it is for the Communist press we organize and train worker correspondents.

The Communist press, like the Communist Party for which it speaks, stands forth as the only clear challenge to the capitalist press and the capitalist class.

The Communist Party is the most intelligent, resolute and disciplined section of the working class. The Communist press is the most militant of all the labor press.

To the Communist press the workers and the working class are always right. It never apologizes for the working class or attempts to reconcile the class conflict. Instead it seeks· to encourage and broaden it.

The worker correspondents of the Communist press therefore are not mere observers and reporters of the workers' struggles. Their stories must not only reflect the life and battles of the working class, but shape their_ lives and struggles. They are not only the pulse of the movement, but the heart as well.

Worker correspondents of the Communist press are not only mirrors in which the class conflicts are reflected, but hammers ·by whose blows these conflicts are welded into one battle line. Their writings must buil "The iron battalions of the proletariat."

Tireless energy is needed by worker correspondents. They secur their information while engaged in the tasks that capitalism allots them Their stories for the most part are·written after the day's toil when bot body and mind are tired. Often they must make special journeys to ge additional facts.

But they can and should write with the hot breath of the struggl still upon them. Sometimes it will seem to them that they are writing wit their own blood.

But they will learn and they will teach the working class that n matter how small a thing it is, if it happens to or affects the workers, i is important.

The first task of worker correspondents is to see every event fron the class angle and to make the workers for whom they write view it th same way. Class pride is the essence of revolutionary journalism and clas pride should shine from every word and line that a worker corresponden writes.
Once more!

'NOTHING THAT HAPPENS TO THE WORKERS IS UNIMPORTANT

The capitalist class and capitalist journalists pay little attention t the daily tyrannies inflicted on the workers. When these things ar noticed, it is only to apologize for, or to justify them. The leaders an social traitors think that only certain things are important, bu Communists know better. It is by paying attention to all the ordinar woes of the working class that Communist journalism demonstrates it class character.

It is only in the Communist press that the workers find a knowledge of their smallest grievances, understanding of the causes of these grievances and the connection of them with their struggles as a class.

The capitalist class rules because it is able to divide the worker and break up their struggles into isolated conflicts. Worker correspondents for the Communist press in every industrial center, in the factories and shops, in unions and fraternal organizations, in rural communities, wherever there are workers, link up these isolated conflicts and give to the working class a correct picture of the world ruled by capitalism because the working class is fighting not as a class, but as individuals and groups.

The Communist press becomes a mass organ reflecting and molding the struggles of the workers in the same proportion that these struggles· are recorded and correctly interpreted by worker correspondents, correspondents who write of the battles of their class as a soldier writes of the battles which he helps to fight. Worker correspondents are WAR correspondents they tell of the class war is its every sector and salient.

An army of worker correspondents means a powerful Communist press.
A powerful Communist press means a powerful Communist Party.

A powerful Communist Party means the Dictatorship of the Working Class-VICTORY FOR THE SOCIAL REVOLUTION.

"Without a Communist press," said the Second Congress of the C. I., "the preparation for the dictatorship of the proletariat is impossible."
We can say, by virtue of the experience gained in our struggles since that time, that without worker correspondents a Communist press is impossible.

Section 2. - Instructions and Suggestions to Worker Correspondents

The material furnished by worker correspondents falls under three general classes :

- (1)   News stories
- (2)   Special articles dealing with one event of importance to the labor and revolutionary movement.
- (3)   Interpretative articles on the nature an(\ progress of the workers' struggles.

NEWS STORIES

- (1)   **Conditions of employment.**
    - (A)   Shop and Job News-Introduction and effect of speed-up system on the workers, tyrannies of foremen, etc.
    - (B)   Methods of hiring workers-physical examinations, record systems-blacklisting.
    - (C)   Wages, hours, state of labor market.

NOTE: The utmost accuracy is needed on these matters.

- (2)   **News of workers' struggles.**
    - (a)   Strikes and lockouts, Election campaigns.
    - (b)   Attitude of city, county, state and federal authorities.
        - (1)   Court actions, injunction, passage of laws against workers, use of po lice, troops, special forcible means of suppression, etc.

- (c) **Form of organizations of capitalists-Political parties.**
    - (1)   Activities of employers' associations, Chambers of Commerce, Commercial clubs, etc.
    - (2)   Use of gunmen, thugs and spies against

workers.

(d)   **Union activities.**
    (1)   Labor movement-Attitude of
        (a)   Towards capitalists.
        (b)   Towards Communists.
        (c)   Towards Negroes.
        (d)   Towards foreign born.

(3)   **Proceedings of Central Labor Council State Federation, Conventions.**

    (a)   Proceedings of local unions-election of officers, wage negotiations, wage agreements, etc.

(4)   **Attitude and activities of churches.**

    (1) Attitude and activities of semi-religious anti-labor organizations like Y. M.C. A., Knights of Columbus, Boy Scouts, etc.

(5)   **Accidents-deaths and injuries of workers.**

(6)   **Housing conditions, rents, evictions.**

(7)   **Activities of middle class fascist and semi-fascist organizations like Klan, Minute Men of Constitution, American Legion, Rotary Clubs, etc.**
    (a)   Attitude and activities of these towards Negroes.

(8)   **Party activities.**
    (a)   Work of Communist Fractions in industrial establislnnents, unions, co-operatives, among farmers, etc.

WRITING NEWS STORIES

(1)   Put the important facts in first paragraph - **WHAT, WHERE, WHEN, WHO, WHY**, should be told in the first paragraph. The arrangement can and should be varied but in pure news stories this rule should seldom be broken.

Sample of this method-

"NEW YORK CITY, May lst-500 LONGSHORE MEN, MEMBERS OF THE INTERNATIONAL LONGSHOREMEN'S ASSOCIATION, LOCAL 999, STRUCK THIS MORNING AT PIER 20, WHEN ORDERED TO LOAD l\IUNITIONS ON THE ADMIRAL LINE BOAT TECUMSEH. THE MUNITIONS WERE FOR THE 1 OLISH COUNTER REVOLUTIONARY ARMY."

(2)   It is better to use short sentences. This method adds to the force of the narrative and is a simple style that is both impressive and easily read.

   (a)   Be accurate. Get the facts straight. Learn to know what is important and put emphasis in this part of the story.

   The Communist press, more than any other press, has to show a detailed and unquestionable knowledge of the struggles of the workers it records. One or two inaccurate statements in a story will be picked on by enemies of the Communists and the working class and used to distract the   attention of the workers from the real issues involved.

(3)   Don't drag comment into a news story by the heels. If the story is written properly it will speak for itself. This does not mean that all interpretation must be eliminated, but it does mean that long dissertations are not necessary and serve merely to detract from the force of the story.

(4)   500 words and less is the best length for ordinary news stories. A. column of the Daily Worker, with the type now used, will take about 660 words. It is therefore evident that most of the news need not run to more than a quarter or half this length. In writing news stories, try to visualize as much as possible, the space they will occupy in the paper. Space in a Communist press is necessarily limited. News stories should give the essentials only. The best news writers write briefly.

Color can be given news stories by a few short sentences dealing with some phase of the subject that typifies the situation reported.

Sample-

"THE STRIKERS LEFT PICKETS ON THE DOCK AND THEN MARCHED TO THEIR HALL SINGING THE INTERNATIONAL AFTER COMMUNIST MEMBERS OF THE UNION HAD MADE SHORT SPEECHES, TELLING THE WORKERS THAT THE MUNITIONS WERE TO BE USED AGAINST THE WORKING CLASS GOVERNMENT OF SOVIET RUSSIA."

(5) Technical details.
   (a) Write on one side of paper only.
   (b) Use typewriter if possible-use triple space
   (c) If stories are written in longhand, leave a half inch between each line.
   (d) Number each page and put at top left hand corner a short title for story that wi]l serve to identify it no matter how the pages may be mixed.
   (e) MARK ENVELOPE-_ "NEWS"- AT LOWER LEFT HAND CORNER.
   (f) Write in sub-heads if story is 200 words and over.
   (g) Mark paragraphs by indenting first line or by marking first line thus L

EXPLANATORY AND ANALYTICAL ARTICLES.

These articles should be a combination of news and interpretation dealing with one subject only. Try to begin with a sentence that will fix the attention of the reader. Don't allow your thoughts to wander. Be convincing.

Write just as if you were talking to one or two workers whom you want to acquaint with the facts and have agreed with your conclusions.

Worker Correspondents

Structure of this type of article:

(1) The premise-concise description of general situation and what you intend to prove.
(2) Give facts and interpretation of them. Make your sustaining argument.
(3) Then draw your conclusions.

These articles should be from 500 to 1,200 words.

General articles on nature of struggle, forces involved and progres of struggle.

An article of this kind should be built up out of the material of a number of news stories. The main purpose of these articles is to connect the different struggles with the general class struggle and the Communist program.

The facts must be clear and there should be a sufficient number of them to avoid the accusation that the conclusions drawn ar based on scanty eddence.

These articles must display a detailed knowledge of conditions o the workers.

The Party policies and its special campaigns and tactics must be studied and the article itself show the application of these to the dail struggle.

The difference between the policies and tactics of the reactionaries, reformists and the Communists must be made clear.

These articles should not run over 2,000 words.

Section 3 - Shop, Factory and Job News

Of all the news which the Communist press carries that of the conditions of the workers in industry is most important.

The working class spends from eight to twelve hours out of the twenty-four at labor from which all joy has long since departed. Modern industry has made of work a deadly, brain sickening monotony-a penalty to be paid for the right to live. The machine drives the worker at an ever-faster speed. The pressure of the capitalist and all his underlings on the backs of the worker becomes heavier. The robbery becomes more and more shameless and protests meet with severe punishment.

Under these conditions the workers in industry sweat and suffer.

What do they think of the giant corporations which dominate their lives? What do they think of the petty bosses who drive them for the capitalists in return for a few cents more added to their day's pay?

What do they think of the ruthless system that scraps human beings more callously than it does the high-priced machines?

What do the workers think of the inhuman manner in which they are numbered and herded in the gigantic hives of modern industry? What do they think of the filthy holes in which they have to work and live?

What do they think of the risks they are forced to take as a part of their job?

What do they think of the company "welfare systems," the hospitals and company doctors and the mad rush of the claim agent to get a release for the company the moment a worker comes back to consciousness after being crushed or mangled?

What do they think of the policemen, the company guards, the spies, the courts, the strike breakers, the detectives, the use of troops, of the whole state machinery of terrorization and suppression organized for and owned by the capitalists?

What do they think of their miserable wages? Of wage-cuts? O unions? Of the lack of unions?

What do the workers propose to do about these things? Do they accept them as inevitable? Are there signs of revolt? What form does their resentment take? In what manner is revolt expressed?

When the Communist press knows and tells of these things it is really a mass organ.

Without worker correspondents it cannot be a true reflection of the lives of the masses.

Such news is not hard to get but to get it one must be a worker. When he writes he becomes a worker correspondent.

Any instructions as to how and what to write, however, can do nothing more than give the reader a general idea of the way of approaching his task. The way to learn to write is to begin to write and after all there is nothing mysterious about the process. Anyone who can think clearly will express himself well in his own language if he gives a little care to certain necessary things.

The principal requirement is to have something to say. Say it as clearly as possible-and then stop. :More speeches and articles are ruined by the speaker or writer continuing after he has exhausted his subject than by anything else.

Let us suppose that a worker has been injured by the lack of a safety device. Tell how the worker was injured, why he was injured, the reason why no safety device was installed, the effect of the accident on the other workers. If there is a union in the shop show how it has neglected to fight for safety devices, if it has, if there is no union show how the need of one is made plain by the accident. But do not preach. Let the facts speak for themselves as much as possible.

Strive to avoid "revolutionary phraseology" as much as possible. Said Lenin:

The revolutionary phrase consists of the repetition of revolutionary slogans, without taking into account the objective circumstances of the present curve of events and the present situation. Wonderfully captivating and intoxicating slogans, without any firm ground beneath them, are the essence of the revolutionary phrase.

"We must never forget that the revolutionary slogans of the Commul}ist Party voiced by the Communist press have connection with the lives of the masses only after systematic preparation of the masses by struggles around their immediate demands.

To throw revolutionary slogans into the labor movement when the masses have not been prepared to support them by Communist agitation, centering around the daily struggles, building the n1ass movement on a firm foundation, is like placing one stick of dynamite under Gibraltar with the expectation of demolishing it.

Says the Agitation and Propaganda department of the Communist International in its criticism of the weaknesses of the Communist press:

Two different things may be comprehended under "revolutionary phrase" in the Communist press. There are Communist papers which invariably follow the principle of employing the strongest and most urgent phraseology which they are capable of compiling, and which give the impression that the writers must have been in a state of high fever.

Viewed as agitation this fails to make any effect upon the masses, repels them, and has besides this the disadvantage that when the newspaper had to deal with some special situation, it finds its vocabulary exhausted.

A second variety ,of the revolutionary phrase is the ceaseless employment of Communist slogans without any internal connection 'With the lives of the workers.

Worker Correspondents

FREQUENTLY THE SIMPLE NARRATION OF FACTS IS MORE EFFECTIVE THAN THE ARTIFICIAL AND WEARISOME REPETITION OF COMMUNIST SLOGANS.

MORE FAITH IN THE THINKING POWER OF THE READERS.

"Less intellectual talk, closer contact with life," said Lenin.

And again:

"Why is it not possible to speak in ten to twenty lines, instead of 200 to 400, of simple, well known, obvious matters, already fairly digested by the masses...? (Lenin, writing on "The Character of Our Newspapers".)

The tasks of the worker correspondents are most important and responsible ones. The workers who read their news stories and articles will judge the press and the party largely by them and the mistake must not be made of thinking that these readers are not critical. They are. They read-and they judge. They look with an eagle eye for errors and even the errors may escape the editors they will not be missed by the workers.

Our press therefore must be as accurate as our program. It is with this knowledge and sense of responsibility flowing from it that the Communist worker correspondent who form the nucleus of the broader groups of non-party correspondents, must approach their job of recording the daily history of the class struggle, popularizing the party organ and thereby building a mass Communist press.

Examples of Worker Correspondence

Appended are a few examples of the sq>ries sent in by worker correspondents and published in the Daily Worker. They are as near perfect as our correspondents are capable of turning out at present, they have been edited very little, some of them not at all, and can be studied to advantage by workers who are just beginning· to write. The quality that all these examples have in common is that they tell of something that has happened affecting large numbers of workers, tell it clearly and in simple language (with one exception which will be explained a little farther on) make certain easily understood suggestions and are entirely devoid of any flamboyant such as was mentioned and criticized in the preceding pages.

The sole exception is the story using the phrase "de mortuis nil nisi bunkum," a clever pun on the old Latin saying "de mortuis nil nisi bonum speak nothing but good of the dead." It would be a hardhearted editor indeed that would prevent a worker correspondent putting over this witty jibe altho foreign phrases are generally to be disregarded.

It will be noticed that these examples deal with the building, toal mining, and steel industries a public function staged by the hangers-on of the capitalist class and party activity. The industrial stories bring in the attitude of the union officials as well as the conditions of the industry, the story of the Harding statue brings in the activity of the boy scouts, the story of party activity brings in something of the conditions of the workers and the attitude of the capitalists and authorities, etc.

These are concrete illustrations of how to link up life with the Communist press and will serve better than many thousand words of instruction.

Steel Worker Victimized by "Safety First" Open Shop and Speed Up i Pittsburgh
By THOMAS (Worker Correspondent)

PITTSBURGH, April 20.-"Safety first" committees have become th pet angel of the steel trust. In reality they are nothing but "open shop propaganda committees trying to force their dope on the workers, nothir is ever given for the benefit of the workers. Here is how it works ou tin the mill where I am employed.

There are paid men who go around the mill every day of th week preaching how much better the place is now than it was te years ago, and try to convince the workers that they are in heaver but it is the opposite, it is the worst hell it is possible to imagine.

"Safety Committee" Always Blames the Workers.

This safety committee is supposed to try to cut down accidents an give reasons when an accident takes place so that men could avoid them i the future. That is what they say they are doing, but there is nothing c the sort. What they do is to put the blame on the shoulders of th workers, for every accident which takes place. Regardless of whose fault i is, the workers are called careless.

There was a young worker fired because he had received a few cut on his hands in one week. An other was fired because he refused t handle heavy bars with an injured hand. There was another worke whose job it was to oil the rolls over which white hot rails run. H could not oil them while the rails were running, so he told th foreman to stop them, which he did, but not long enough for the worke to finish the job with the result that a hot rail went clean thru hi body and killed him.

At the next "safety meeting" a paid speaker of the compan came and stated that a man had been killed, and as much as th company regretted it, it is mainly thru his own carelessness and tha he had no business in that spot; this, altho he had been ordered there b the foreman, and then the speaker went on to state the difference in th accidents now and ten years ago.

"All Time Want More Work."

A good many of the foreign born workers can see that the safety meeting is a speed-up meeting. I spoke to one today and altho he could not understand the English language very good or even speak it. I asked him what he thought of the meetings he said, "All time want more work." So you see the impression that he got.

The company has its spies all over the plant who will report any talk of a union that they hear, and some excuse is immediately found to fire the one who advocates organization.

The wages are so low that the workers have barely enough to live on and if any sickness takes place they have to trust to charity of others. If you are injured too bad to be able to walk to work, the company will send the ambulance to fetch you and take you home again in the evening in order to keep dis content at a minimum.

The main point is they are afraid the men will organize once again to better their conditions. They have done it once and they will do it again.

Bricklayers' Officials Work for the Bosses

By UNION BRICKLAYER (Worker Correspondent)

NEW YORK CITY, April-At a ·conference of the building industry held here pertaining to the supposed tie up of $22,000,000 worth of building construction, it was brought out plainly and positively to the notice of the workers, how the bricklayers' and plasterers' "representatives" sell them to both the sub-contractors and .general contractors.

This happens whenever it chances to meet with these representatives' financial approval, as in the southern affair, and not in the interest of the workers. As William Bowen, president of the Bricklayers and Plasterers union stated at the said conference, he was working for the sub-contractors interest, and not for the union, as quoted in the New York World.

Union bricklayers recall the scabby affair of the same bunch o labor fakers, Bowen, Breece and company, when they used the unior members of Local 37 of New York City as scabs against the Local o Rochester, N. Y., paying their fare to Rochester to scab on their fellow workers for the interest of their masters-who paid them well for the faithful performance of their "duty."

Again, union bricklayers and plasterers recall Vice-President Thornton's action in January, 1924, selling Local No. 1 members of Philadelphia to Mr. Adkins, a scab contractor.

And again union men recall the Boston Open Shop Drive in 1921 when the official gang allowed the big boss, whom they pretended to fight, to establish the open shop on our eastern local unions.

It is laughable to think that these labor fakers can be bought so cheaply by the masters and still expect the bricklayers and plasterers to look up to them as labor leaders, when the very same master who buys them so cheaply tells the world thru their capitalist papers that they are strikebreakers.

The New York Journal of April 17, 1925, stated that the Bricklayers and Plasterers International Union imported their so-called union men into Syracuse, New York, to break a strike and prevent the workers there from getting a living wage.

The officials of this union are among the champion strikebreakers or the U. S. A.

Marble Statue Generates Hot Air for 2,500 De Mortuis Nihil Nisi Bunkum
By WORKER CORRESPONDENT

SEATTLE, Wash., April 19. A monument to the late President Harding was unveiled here. It stands in Woodland Park where Harding gave the oath of allegiance to 30,000 boy scouts, and was presented by the Elks lodge. Only 2,500 were present this time, the reputation of Harding having been sadly tarnished since he was here.

Three Elks presented the monument to the city, and two professional politicians, acting for the city accepted it. The boy scouts had the honor (?) of paying for it.

Among the bunk peddled out by the speakers were such statements as: "nothing better can be done by the Elks than to teach love of country to boys . . . Harding was one of the greatest examples of the greatness of American manhood" (this from a democrat, ex-socialist-wonder what he thinks of Daugherty, Forbes, etc.) ".... The American people took him from their midst and exalted him ... because he was so common" (common what?) and was it "the American people" who chose him in that room at the Blackstone hotel at two o'clock one morning in June, 1920?

"Let each of us dedicate ourselves anew to our country, to respect its laws and defend its liberty" (this from a hard boiled republican congressman who has been one of the most consistent foes of the workers in congress.)

Needless to say there were many revealing incidents of Harding's life that the speakers forgot to mention. "De mortuis nihil nisi bunkum" was their motto. And so Teapot Dome, the house of K. St., Charley Forbes, etc. were not mentioned.

Our Party Activity
The Spirit of the Communists in Northern Minnesota.

In a country where the boundless, gloomy forests of Northern Minnesota repeat the angry song of the frozen Canadian hills, together with the spring, grows and increases the influence of Communism. The bosses and their lackeys, exasperated, beat the alarm. When, five months ago, their tocal news papers wrote that the red propaganda, after the big miners' strike in 1917, is dead in the iron range (altho in the same time we organized our English branch in South Hibbing) they were celebrating the victory of the reaction. Poor bosses! Soon their illusions had to die and the newspaper pointed out the opposite, altho their police were watching the actions of the Communist leaders very close.

The fifty-two branches in Saint Louis county, the heart of the mining industry, ar awaking, their activity has been stimulated by the trip of Comrade C. A. Hathaway, district organizer. The language branches are uniting their efforts instead of being disunited as before.

It is natural that in such a state of affairs their activity will be weakened. There was no consciousness that the growing of our party and its influence depend on our co-operative actions.

After the first public meeting in Chisholm I was surprised at hearing a few unknown workers calling me: "Hello, Comrade."

The result was workers joined our party. Each Communist effort, each action is not without results and knowing that we have to double our energy.

Of course, the reaction don't sleep and that is why we have to be ready to meet it.

Is there any power to stop a real Communist? No. There is a fresh example-Comrade Stainslav Lanzutsky.

GEO. ZAICKOV.

Union Officials Ignore Miners' Job Complaints
Agreement Works Only One Way in Mines
By A MINER (Worker Correspondent)

BENTLEYVILLE, Pa., April 20-Many of the favorable conditions formerly prevailing have been lost by the miners in District Five since the officials signed the last agreement. The excuse given for not fighting the company is bad times and fear that the company will shut down the mines. On the Bentleyville Branch there are ten mines, only four of which are working, but still these cowardly officials say it is better than nothing.

The first condition that the miners lost was a rule in the mines that if a man worked in a wet place he received $5.00 extra in two weeks. One day the company cut off this extra $5.60 and the men refused to work unless they could get their well earned money.

Wet Work Not Paid as Agreed.

They took it up with their committee but failed to reach any agreement with the bosses. They then took it up with the board members and were given the decision that if the bosses wouldn't pay, that they would have to put the men in dry places. This the men accepted right away. The pit boss put them in other places and- hired new men who had been eut of work about six months. These men were glad to get jobs under any conditions and none of them received one cent extra for working in water. That was the settlement madeby our "good" officials.

The Drivers' Complaint ignored.

Our drivers had been used to start at 6:30 in the morning to leave the stable. The mine developed so far that the drivers could not reach their working places at seven and the company fired one driver for not starting at 7:00 o'clock as the agreement called for. In fact some of these drivers had a good hour's way to, travel underground before they reached their working places.

This was also taken up with the company without any result, so they called upon their board member for help. He notified them that if they could not reach their working places at seven they should leave the stable earlier or else he could not do anything for them in case they got fired and now the boss takes care of the firing part.

Waiting for Cars-To Help the Boss.

The four mines still operating are only working from two to four days a week, so the bosses are trying to get as much coal out on these days as possible. To increase their tonnage they have some picked men working every day, mostly the bosses' favored men. They fill all the empty cars in the mine from the coal knocked down by the miners the day before and when the latter come to work they have to wait two to four hours before they get their first car.

The miners called a special meeting to stop this practice and also to stop the method used by the bosses of doubling up two men in one place. They elected a committee to meet with the bosses, but as usual they failed to get any results.

Again they asked their board member to come and help them in their fight but he told them to do the best they could, he could not help them because the company would shut down the mine if they stop these practices. The company refused to give the miners any satisfaction because they know they can get much more favorable decisions from the officials.

No Protection from the Union.

Every day some new bad condition and not a word of protest from our officials because they say we have an agreement for three years and we should be glad we are working. However the miners are beginning to see the point and getting ready for the fight, if the officials will not fight the miners are apt to take matters into their own hands.

Building the Communist Press

News of the workers' struggles is of no value unless it is read by the workers.

The Communist press and the Communist Party is not, in the liberal fashion, conducting a laboratory experiment to determine the extent of tyranny and the amount of it the worker can stand. It is not interested in the grievances of the workers merely for humanitarian reasons.

It publishes the news of the oppressions practiced by the capitalists, not to create a sensation but for other workers to read and understand so they will hate the system that produces such tyranny. The Communist press is working for the revolution, it is trying to arouse and inspire the workers to fight.

Of equal importance then to the gathering of news is the distribution of it. A worker correspondent must be not only an observer and chronicler, but a medium thru which flows back to the workers whose struggles he relates, the story and Communist interpretation of those struggles.

To read about themselves is a new experience for most workers. To read about themselves as the actors in the great drama of the class struggle, as soldiers in the class war, is an experience they can get only from the Communist press.

They may not show any startling proofs of gratitude at first but worker correspondents will find that with the Communist press telling of the actual everyday events in the mines and factories, building circulation for it will not be a difficult task.

Whenever there is a story about a particular shop or of the activities or grievances of a particular group of workers, the worker correspondent must see that these workers get the paper.

They will read it and as they find out that it is really what it claims to be, the fighting organ of the whole working class, they will give it their confidence and support.

This is the only way in which the Communist press can be rooted deeply in the masses, rooted so deeply that it can fight the battles of the workers no matter what suppressive measures the capitalist state invokes to silence it.

Once established among the millions who toil the Communist press can devote all its attention to preparing the dictatorship of the proletariat.

Appendix

The Character Of Our Newspapers by Vladimir Lenin

Delivered: 8 November, 1918

Far too much space is being allotted to political agitation on outdated themes—to political ballyhoo—and far too little to the building of the new life, to the facts about it.

Why instead of turning out 200-400 lines, don't we write twenty or even ten lines on such simple, generally known, clear topics with which the people are already fairly well acquainted, like the foul treachery of the Mensheviks—the lackeys of the bourgeoisie—the Anglo-Japanese invasion to restore the sacred rights of capital, the American multimillionaires baring their fangs against Germany, etc., etc.? We must write about these things and note every new fact in this sphere, but we need not write long articles and repeat old arguments; what is needed is to condemn in just a few lines, "in telegraphic style", the latest manifestation of the old, known and already evaluated politics.

The bourgeois press in the "good old bourgeois times" never mentioned the "holy of holies"—the conditions in privately-owned factories, in the private enterprises. This custom fitted in with the interests of the bourgeoisie. We must radically break with it. We have not broken with it. So far our type of newspaper has not changed as it should in a society in transition from capitalism to socialism.

Less politics. Politics has been "elucidated" fully and reduced to a struggle between the two camps: the insurrectionary proletariat and the handful of capitalist slave owners (with the whole. gang, right down to the Mensheviks and others). We may, and, I repeat, we must, speak very briefly about these politics.

More economics. But not in the sense of "general" discussions, learned reviews, intellectual plans and similar piffle, for, I regret to say, they are all too often just piffle and nothing more. By economics we mean the gathering, careful checking and study of the facts of the actual organisation of the new life. Have real successes been achieved by big factories, agricultural communes, the Poor Peasants' Committees, and local Economic Councils in building up the new economy? What, precisely, are these successes? Have they been verified? Are they not fables, boasting, intellectual proinises ("things are moving", "the plan has been drawn up", "we are getting underway", "we now vouch for", "there is undoubted improvement", and other charlatan phrases of which "we" are such masters)? How have the successes been achieved? What must be done to extend them?

Where is the black list with the names of the lagging factories which since nationalisation have remained models of disorder, disintegration, dirt, hooliganism and parasitism? Nowhere to be found. But there are such factories. We shall not be able to do our duty unless we wage war against these "guardians of capitalist traditions". We shall be jellyfish, not Communists, as long as we tolerated such factories. We have not learned to wage the class struggle in the newspapers as skilfully as the bourgeoisie did. Remember the skill with which it hounded its class enemies in the press, ridiculed them, disgraced them, and tried to sweep them away. And we? Doesn't the class struggle in the epoch of the transition from capitalism to socialism take the form of safeguarding the interests of the working class against the few, the groups and sections of workers who stubbornly cling to capitalist traditions and continue to regard the Soviet state in the old way: work as little and as badly as they can and grab as much money as possible from the state. Aren't there many such scoundrels, even among the compositors in Soviet printing works, among the Sormovo and Putilov workers, etc.? How many of them have we found, how many have we exposed and how many have we pilloried?

The press is silent. And if it mentions the subject at all it does so in a stereotyped, official way, not in the manner of a revolutionary press, not as an organ of the dictatorship of a class demonstrating that the resistance of the capitalists and of the parasites-the custodians of capitalist traditions will be crushed with an iron hand.

The same with the war. Do we harass cowardly or inefficient officers? Have we denounced the really bad regiments to the whole of Russia? Have we "caught" enough of the bad types who should be removed from the army with the greatest publicity for unsuitability, carelessness, procrastination, etc.? We are not yet waging an effective, ruthless and

Worker Correspondents

truly revolutionary war against the specific wrongdoers. We do very little to educate the people by living, concrete examples and models taken from all spheres of life, although that is the chief task of the press during the transition from capitalism to communism. We give little attention to that aspect of everyday life inside the factories, in the villages and in the regiments where, more than anywhere else, the new is being built, where attention, publicity, public criticism, condemnation of what is bad and appeals to learn from the good are needed most.

Less political ballyhoo. Fewer highbrow discussions. Closer to life. More attention to the way in which the workers and peasants are actually building the new in their everyday work, and more verification so as to ascertain the extent to which the new is communistic.

N. Lenin

William F. Dunne

PEOPLE'S SCHOOL FOR MARXIST LENINIST STUDIES
http://www.psmls.org/

Every 2nd & 4th Thursday night
8:30pm EST / 7:30pm CST / 6:30pm MST / 5:30pm PST

Communist schools and universities have been a mainstay in the Communist movement for generations.

In the early years in the US the American communist movement set up workers book shops and schools, such as the workers school in New York City. During the popular front years, the Communist Party (CP) set up the Jefferson school for social research, named after Thomas Jefferson this was in accordance with the CP's positioning at the time which stated, "communism is 20th century Americanism."

During the McCarthy period, the Jefferson school was forced to close. From the late 1970s into the early 80s the People's School for Marxist Studies became a center for pro-Soviet and anti-Trotskyite knowledge in the American left.

Today we are taking the bold step of rebuilding Marxist Leninist schools in the US.

Through the use of various extension courses throughout the country and affiliated study groups, the school continues the task of ideologically educating workers including the unemployed, oppressed people, and youth in the science of Marxism-Leninism and its application in various struggles.

One of the school's objectives is to give working people tools needed in pushing the labor movement away from social democracy and economism and towards military class struggle trade unionism.

Worker Correspondents

A New Beginning for U.S. Communists, Founded May Day 2014

Program

Points of Unity

PCUSA 1st Congress

Constitution

https://partyofcommunistsusa.org

MOVEMENT FOR PEOPLE'S DEMOCRACY

PRINCIPLES AND OBJECTIVES

To unite all democratic minded, peace loving people in the USA into a national united front against fascism and war.

To provide a people's' response to state sponsored terrorism and violence in our communities.

To demand an agenda for social justice

To fight corruption

To demand accountability and transparency from our elected representatives.

To bring corporate domination of our economy to an end.

To establish people's' councils in every community with authority to enforce laws that protect the people from abuse of authority.

www.movement4peoplesdemocracy.org

Our Mission
The aim of all Friends of the Soviet People is international cooperation in building socialism and solidarity with the anti-imperialist forces of the world who are struggling against U.S. Imperialism - the main enemy of humanity.

Our History
U.S. Friends of the Soviet People is the successor to the National Council of American - Soviet Friendship (NCASF) Started in 1918 as "Hands Off Russia" Committees.

usfriendsofthesovietpeople.org
Email: angelo4ny@aol.com
(718) 979-6563

http://www.usfriendsofthesovietpeople.org

William F. Dunne

North American Region

Post Office Box 1641, Manhattanville Station, New York, NY 10027 *E-mail: joseph@labortoday.us

Labor Today is published by the **Labor United for Class Struggle (LUCS)**, a nationwide caucus of union and non-represented workers. Our mission is to unite the working class to fight against the power of transnational capital. Currently only 11% of the U.S. workforce is organized into unions. Most of these workers are employed in the public sector, and are legally denied the right to strike. The most militant of these workers are the postal workers employed by the U.S. Postal Service. For this reason, they are under attack. However, they are not the only ones.

The attacks on the public sector and its workforce are part of a larger plan developed years ago by Milton Friedman and the University of Chicago School of Business. The plan is referred to as neoliberalism and its main feature is austerity. Reducing the number of federal , state, and municipal employees and cutting pensions and Social Security are the first part of the plan which President Ronald Reagan called "starving the beast". Under this plan, all government services are virtually eliminated with the exception of the military, and the Executive, Judicial, and Legislative Branches of government. This is also called Social Darwinism, or survival of the fittest.

Our mission with Labor Today and the LUCS caucus is to unite all of Labor, to give them a voice regardless of industry or type of work without regard to status: union or unrepresented. We provide assistance to the Walmart workers, the Fight for $15 and a union and other efforts. We are transnational and we support the mission and policies of the World Federation of Trade Unions (WFTU).

http://www.labortoday.us

The **League of Young Communists USA** is the Communist Youth Organization of the Party of Communists USA.

The Party of Communists USA traces its roots from dropped clubs of the Communist Party USA. Members of the New York Transport Workers Union club, the Arts & Entertainment CPUSA club, the Staten Island club, the Buffalo NY club, the Los Angeles club and various comrades scattered around the country, such as in California, Hawaii, Illinois, Minnesota and Texas, were the original founders of the Party of Communists USA. The PCUSA and the LYCUSA are dedicated to upholding Marxism-Leninism, scientific socialism, internationalism and Socialism-Communism. Our focus is on class struggle, workers' rights, and creating the conditions for a socialist revolution. The PCUSA established the League of Young Communists USA as the successor to the Young Communist League of the CPUSA, which was officially disbanded in 2015. The YCL had been in existence for almost one hundred years.

http://www.leagueofyoungcommunistsusa.org

www.ingramcontent.com/pod-product-compliance
Lightning Source LLC
Chambersburg PA
CBHW061232280526
45784CB00006B/2740